BLUFF YOUR WAY IN

P.R.

BASIL SAUNDERS
&
ALEXANDER C. RAE

RAVETTE BOOKS

Published by Ravette Books Limited
3 Glenside Estate, Star Road
Partridge Green, Horsham,
West Sussex RH13 8RA
(0403) 710392

First printed 1991
Reprinted 1992

Series Editor – Anne Tauté

Cover design – Jim Wire
Printing & Binding – Cox & Wyman Ltd.
Production – Oval Projects Ltd.

The Bluffer's Guides are based on
an original idea by Peter Wolfe.

CONTENTS

INTRODUCTION

The great advantage of public relations for the bluffer is that nobody has a firm idea of what a PR person actually does all day long.

You may gain some inkling from these pages. If so, don't pass it on. Keep them guessing, that's the motto. Otherwise, where should we all be?

Public relations is *all* bluff. It is bluffery elevated to the status of a profession. By the time you have finished this short course, you will be as well qualified to practise in public relations as a number of others, not themselves professionals, who are currently doing so. We shall, of course, be telling you how to make money out of it, which is the only trick worth knowing.

What makes life exciting is that, in public relations, people expect you to bluff. They know you are bluffing. You tell them you are bluffing. But you go on bluffing just the same.

Public relations is the Happiness Business. Grand openings. Royal visits. Knighthoods. Freebies. Scientific breakthroughs. Record financial results. You need never ride in a bus or on the underground again. You will explain to The Client that your time spent waiting for a bus would cost him a good deal more than the taxi, which of course will be charged to him (plus a percentage).

PR people will keep telling you (and you must start saying it) that public relations ranges much wider than 'mere' press relations, 'getting little bits into the papers.' They say this because getting The Client even into the News in Brief is really quite tricky (though we shall be telling you how to do it). It is wise to divert attention to other areas of communication, such as Parliament and the City, where results are less readily measurable.

"I've been doing a lot of *iceberg* work for my clients," a distinguished PR consultant used to inform everybody, unsmiling. He meant that what was to be found beneath the surface was seven times as great as what was visible.

The same consultant issued a brochure entitled *How Are You Tomorrow?* to try to catch clients. Tomorrow is the ideal day for the bluffer. It keeps moving on.

THE BASICS

The Client

In Public Relations, The Client is the person that you do it *for*. The world at large represents the people that you will do it *to*. The Client is the person that makes the whole game possible.

To find a client, look for a managing director who is so preoccupied with the out-of-stock list, the wage claim and the boiler that is about to blow up that he has no time for long-term, in-depth thinking. You will purport to provide this for him.

There is probably some European Community legislation in the pipeline which, if implemented, will put his industry out of business. You can track the progress of this measure for him through all its stages. It could occupy you for years.

The point about The Client is that, while you and I get up to a lot of things, both in the office and outside it, his whole life is devoted to iron filings or ball bearings or whatever his business might be. He lives and breathes them for twenty-four hours of the day.

Do not imagine that, after a solemn meeting in the agency, The Client might like to join you in the pub, to put it all behind him and let his hair down a bit. He will talk about iron filings there too. And he will be restless for fear he will miss that evening's meeting of the Ball Bearing Association.

It is important to realise that clients are, by nature, the most conservative and timid of creatures. They like to picture themselves as risk-taking wheeler-dealers who live on a knife edge. But in the final analysis, they are more interested in not making a mistake than in pulling off the greatest publicity coup of all time. The only people not to be aware of this self-evident truth are clients themselves.

Above all, do not ever tell The Client that you cannot see him on Wednesday because you will be occupied with the business of Another Client. Like spouses, clients may not show that they love you, but they become very jealous if they think that you love someone else.

Who's In, Who's Out

There are basically two areas of PR bluffing. There is the in-house PR person, on the staff of the organisation whose story is to be told. Then there is the bluffer in the specialist PR agency or the 'independent' PR consultant operating on his or her own. In the course of your career, as you 'career' from one crisis to another, you will probably spend some time on both sides of the fence.

There is not really all that much difference between the two, merely a shift of emphasis and a change in behaviour. Agency PR people will always try to be somewhere else. In-house PR people have to stay at home and watch over what they've got.

If you are appointed to an in-house position insist on retaining an outside agency. This means that they will do all the dogsbodying instead of you and will always be on hand to take the blame.

On the same principle, a consultant gaining a new account will demand an in-house PRO for purposes of 'liaison' and, in a spirit of generosity, to furnish more jobs for the bluffers. The more bluffing that is going on, the better we shall all survive.

The in-house PR person who owes his job to the agency, and may have been selected by them, might start to imagine that he is himself The Client but the agency knows different. They have not selected him as the person who calls the shots.

If you are the in-house PR person, the whole of the rest of your organisation acts as The Client. You will need an outside agency if only to supply you with alibis.

Confusing the issue, as we all must, you, as the in-house anchor man, may choose to be styled as the company's resident PR Consultant. It is a useful designation: you don't want to give people the impression that you are actually going to do any *work*.

Within the agency, almost everyone will be called a consultant. In-house, you are more likely to choose some such title as Director of Public Relations, leaving those outside the company with the vague suspicion that you just might be on the board.

Whatever your title, do not be tempted actually to direct anybody. Empire building may seem too easy; there is no limit to the amount of activity that could be conducted under the heading of public relations. You could build up a whole Department with a photographers' studio, a film unit and a print section. However, not only will a whole department (or Division) present too large a target when the time comes for cuts, but the members of staff will all be busy having colds and having babies and will want to tell you about them.

It will be as much as you can accomplish to get any bluffing done at all.

Equipment

The one piece of vital equipment you need is the draft stamp.

Any document that you produce is to be stamped

DRAFT in large black letters. If The Client rings to say that what you have written is a lot of hot air, you tell him that what you have sent is no more than a discussion document, the first attempt ever to express a new inspiration in terms of cognitive thought. It was marked 'Draft', didn't he notice?

You say that you 'especially value his input.' You then have another go and try to get it right. He has probably contemptuously quoted one or two phrases, so at least you now know what not to keep in.

If he makes no adverse comment, you print out the document again and circulate it without the draft stamp. The Client may even have rung ecstatically to report that your inspiration has truly got through to him. You never know.

If you are an outside consultant, particularly if you are operating on your own, you might like an array of clocks on your wall, showing the time in various world centres (Tokyo, Sydney, Los Angeles) where you might be supposed to have branch offices.

What hour these clocks show does not matter much. Nobody can work out on the spot what time it ought to be in Kuala Lumpur. But it does matter that the clocks should all show the same minutes past the hour. Otherwise The Client will suspect that you do not know what you are doing and will start to query your invoices.

You also want room on your wall for a number of pictures, each one showing you talking to a recognisable public figure (President Nixon, Madonna, the Dalai Lama). A good photo-finisher should be able to fix these for you with the skilful application of an air brush.

PR Types

There are several distinct types of PR person, all of which have found themselves a comfortable niche. The types are based on what job you did before you came into PR. You have to have done something before you came into PR. If you are straight from school or have never bothered to work before in your life, you will need to make something up.

No-one in public relations started in the business. Children want to be astronauts or nurses. Nobody says to the careers master: "My real ambition is to be a public relations officer for a multi-national industrial conglomerate."

All PR people seem to have fallen into the job entirely by accident. This applies especially to the 'ex-journalist' type who will go to a great deal of trouble to whip up a story to prove that he never wanted to be a PR man and that he dreams of going back to being chief copy-taster for the *Dufftown Bugle*.

PR is one of the few professions which you are positively required to enter later in life. If you were to try "I've been a chartered surveyor for the last fifteen years but I think I'd make a good brain surgeon" at an NHS interview, you would instantly be out on your ear. But try "I just seem to have tired of the world of circus escapology and I feel I need a new challenge" in a PR interview and you will find you are half way there.

There are a number of jobs in PR that a school-leaver could get. Give these a wide berth. PR is only fun if you are in a senior position. With so many top-flight bluffers already in the profession anyone junior is liable to find themselves doing a lot of work while a more senior bluffer takes all the credit.

There are only a few basic PR types. Simply choose

the role that suits your personality best. If you are working in-house, you will have to be more or less consistent, picking one type and sticking to it. In a consultancy you may require to change your type from one hour to the next according to the different clients you are working for on the same day.

Each type dresses differently. It is always a danger, especially amongst in-house PR people, to think that you can get away with dressing like others in the office. You represent to your colleagues the embodiment of that ethereal concept, the Creative. You are something exotic, exciting and slightly dangerous. You won't last long if you turn up on your first day dressed like a sales rep.

Ex-journalist Type

This is by far the most common type, based on the game-keeper turned poacher theory. It is argued that after years of being on the receiving end of PR propaganda, you should be adept at being able to churn it out yourself.

However, this theory fails to recognise the way journalists approach press releases. In the event that there is a space to be filled by PR material, it is usually chosen by one of two methods:

1. because it has a suitable photograph

2. because it is the right length.

Neither of these methods actually involves journalists in reading the material and, in fact, they will often go to great lengths to avoid reading it. Luckily employers don't realise this when they employ ex-journalists.

The essential elements of a (supposed) ex-journalist's dress are:

a) a suit that looks as though you have slept in it for three nights

b) scuffed shoes

c) a tie with a beer stain on it.

Ex-army Type

Army officers retire early, usually without any useful qualifications, and have to find a job where no experience or ability is necessary. What better career than public relations?

The ex-army role is normally only played in order to get a job with a company that is pathologically suspicious of public relations.

There is something very reassuring to the average chief executive about seeing a group of journalists marched around a press visit like a bunch of squaddies. If you pick the right firm, you need only award yourself a rank in a good regiment (nothing below Major), buy a tweed suit, polish your shoes and turn up for the interview.

Thereafter, always announce yourself as Major ****
and encourage people to refer to you as "the Major." You could promote yourself to Brigadier for your next job, on the strength of your added experience.

Ex-graduate Type

Always go for a good degree at a good university. Even if you have a first class honours in Communications at Hull University, it is better to opt for Languages at a real university. Don't worry if you only have two

O levels and a Life Saving Medal. Although you will be required to fill pages of your CV with details of your qualifications, never has an interviewer said "I wonder if I could have a quick look at your degree?"

If you are the ex-graduate type, you should dress the way students dressed 20 years ago when your interviewer was at university. It would be extremely dangerous to dress the way students do today.

Other roles you might like to play are:

Scion of the Aristocracy

In the old days, the eldest son took the title, the second son went into the army and the third into the church. Nowadays the third son (or daughter) will more often go into public relations: the hours are better and you don't need to wear a uniform.

This is a particularly good job for tall women with an upper-class accent. They can spend their time arranging dinner parties for the managing director and choosing the colour scheme for the head office foyer.

Old Faithful

This is one of the most difficult ones to swing. You have to persuade your potential employer that you have been on the payroll of his company for the last 20 years, doing a dreary job very conscientiously.

Such people are not bad enough to sack and not good enough to put into any position of authority. They are given a public relations post (or at least title) because:

a) they know everything that goes on in the company

b) they will pay an unhealthy attention to detail

c) they are not dangerous.

In reality, each of these reasons is enough to preclude them from public relations but you can't tell some people anything.

Interviews

There are huge differences between an interview for a job in a PR agency and one for an in-house PR post.

The interviewer in the agency could not care less if you can do the job as long as you are not a threat to his or her career. The interviewers for the in-house post are desperately keen that you should be able to do the job but have only the flimsiest idea of what it entails.

Note that for the in-house position it will be interviewers in the plural. You may be interviewed by seven people one after the other or by 12 all at the same time. Be sure that you will be interrogated by every executive they can find. Each will have a different, though vague, concept of what public relations involves.

Watch out for the 'What do you see as the function of public relations?' question. You must never give them a straight answer to this for fear you might provide a clue. There are certain questions that they would like answered, though they cannot think of the right way to ask them. Try to insert these answers into the conversation:

1. I know all the things that PR people are supposed to do and I will do them without having to ask you what they are (although I am sure that you would know what they are if I did ask you).

2. I will not do anything on my own initiative but will check with everyone in the organisation before I issue a word on any aspect of the company.

3. When things go really wrong, I'll make sure you don't have to speak to the press.

4. Although I'm a highly creative kind of person, underneath I'm just as boring as you are.

5. When I get corporate entertainment tickets for the cup final / rugby international / Wimbledon / Grand Prix, I will make sure that you get one.

And don't forget, when asked if you have a clean driving licence, the answer is not "Yes. I keep it in a plastic case."

The major disadvantage of working in an agency is that you have to look enthusiastic and sincere. Any good bluffer can look enthusiastic and/or sincere for quite long periods of time. But to do it permanently is very tiring around the sides of the face and can cause severe muscle cramp and premature wrinkles.

Your CV for the agency should show five A levels and a good degree from a good university. This will naturally be a better education than that of your interviewer (though not perhaps a better one than he claimed in his CV) but it will not prove a threat. Education is a complete irrelevance in the agency world. What it does is allow the consultancy to boast that they have on their staff someone with an honours degree in Press Releases from Old Queens' College, Oxbridge.

Your job history should show that you have been employed by five PR agencies, each job lasting roughly two years. Claim any longer than this and the interviewer will become suspicious. You are safe to quote real agencies as long as you claim to have worked for them at least three years ago. There will be no-one left there who is able to deny it.

MEDIA RELATIONS

Having a good relationship with the media is vital for the modern PR bluffer. The process of creating this good relationship is called media relations – a term you can use to cover all the time in the week you can't account for otherwise.

In the old days there was the press agent. There still is, but PR people are unlikely to call themselves that. They shrink from the idea that they are no more than publicists, though a publicist is just what The Client wants. You will educate him to know better.

Media Relations is the most obvious part of PR and the bit that is easiest to explain and even to justify. It is also the bit that is most fun, though this is a word you must never use in front of The Client.

You tell The Client that media relations, and indeed all PR, is 'two-way' communication. You are taking journalists to lunch, though The Client is picking up the tab (plus a percentage), so that you can learn at first hand what the journalists want and how they perceive The Client. In reality they don't want anything at all and they never give The Client a thought.

Press Conferences

The Press Conference is possibly the most important tool at the PR bluffer's disposal. It gives you the opportunity of doing the one thing that ensures you a successful and long-standing relationship with your clients. It allows you to put the fear of God into them and convince them that they cannot live without you.

Getting the journalists there should be no problem. You simply fill in a number on the form of the outside press distribution agency (charge it to The Client) and their computer will send a letter, addressed by name, to every Mining Correspondent or whatever category you choose.

The letter should give a suitably baffling outline of what the story is going to be so that they will have to come along to sort it out. Journalists go to press conferences to meet each other. As soon as you know one or two are coming, tell the rest.

However lavishly you entertain the press, someone else will always go one better. Journalists will praise your champagne but tell you that your competitor (worse still, The Client's competitor) gave them quails' eggs. The best ploy is to go to the other extreme and make a play of providing simple, wholesome fare so as not to corrupt the channels of communication. If feasible, serve something green and recycled, so long as it does not actually smell.

You can always have a bottle of whisky and some smoked salmon in a side room for other members of your consultancy and for your cronies. Not for The Client, naturally. He must never see you enjoying yourself or the whole game will be up.

Don't give the journalists a drink until they have got the story. If you offer a drink on arrival, a party atmosphere will develop and soon they will not care whether they get a story or not.

Q & As

You will spend far more time rehearsing The Client for his part in the press conference than the event itself.

The first stage in schooling The Client involves introducing the idea of Questions and Answers, or Q &

As as you will casually call them. You tell The Client that you will work out a list of questions he is liable to be asked, together with suitable answers. This, you explain, is so that he will not be caught out by unexpected or particularly difficult challenges.

You are, of course, being rather economical with the truth. The Client does not want to hear the kind of question that he really will get, such as 'Where is the Gents?' and 'Is the bar open yet?'

Use your inside knowledge of the company to think up the most mind-numbingly frightening questions you can imagine: "Is it true that your baby food is radio-active?" or "What are you planning to do when the next tranche of the company's debt repayment becomes due in three months' time?" Usually after no more than 20 to 30 minutes of rehearsal The Client will stop sobbing, and within an hour he will become quite docile.

Watch out you don't go too far and put The Client off press conferences for ever. This would mean missing out on a pleasant morning and lunch-time and having to spend those hours at 'work'.

The remaining obstacle is that, when you get to the press conference, the truly awkward questions are never asked, principally because nobody can be bothered. The one or two keen young reporters who would like to look smart never seem to know enough to put together a tricky question. The others are unwilling to ask a question because they know a long, boring answer from the chairman will delay indefinitely the opening of the bar.

It is necessary therefore to take one of the journalists aside on arrival and program him to ask three of the questions you have rehearsed. It is worthwhile getting him to ask them virtually word for word as previously presented to The Client. This means that:

19

a) The Client is far more likely to recognise the question

b) he will give the answer you prepared without your prompting, and will look smooth and professional, perhaps for the only time in his life

c) it will prove how well you have your finger on the pulse of the press.

When you are training clients to answer questions, warn them not to try to be clever. Quote the story of the bishop arriving in New York who was asked by reporters if he was going to visit any night clubs.

"*Are* there any night clubs in New York?" he replied cannily. Next day the papers came out with Bishop's First Question: Are There Any Night Clubs In New York?

The "Then the dancing girls will parachute from a hot air balloon" Trick

While you are planning the press conference you can come up with as many outrageous ideas as your fevered imagination will allow. For instance "And at this point we break off from the prepared speeches and a spot-light picks out a baby elephant riding a bicycle on a tightrope" or "As every journalist walks through the door he should be presented with a live llama."

The Client will agree whole-heartedly, thrilled at the adventurous and inventive way his company will be presented. He will then lie awake in bed for the next three weeks worrying about the logistics of getting four hundred live llamas into the banqueting suite of a smart hotel.

Having let him stew for a suitable period you decide

that it would be far better to give each journalist a picture of a live llama and a pen with the company logo on it. The Client will be so grateful he will not notice how disastrously dull the final event turns out to be.

The Name Badge Ruse

Nervous newcomers to the PR game may try to avoid the use of those little badges with everyone's name on them, so much loved by people who have press conferences. The seasoned bluffer insists that these badges be used. You explain that it is so that the chairman won't waste his time chatting to the 'man from the *Sun*' when he should be having an in depth discussion with the 'man from the *Financial Times*'. However, the badges are worn to hide the fact that 90 per cent of the journalists at the press conference aren't remotely involved with the subject being conferenced, and the other 10 per cent aren't journalists.

You should have badges made out for imaginary people from every quality newspaper and TV network you can think of. Clients always seem to read these names before anyone arrives. Don't worry that they will notice there *isn't* a man from the *Times*. Once the press conference begins, clients seem only able to count, never to read.

Luckily this is helped by the fact that journalists insist on either:

a) not wearing the badge

b) wearing the badge upside down

c) wearing a badge of someone more interesting who hasn't turned up yet.

The Client will eventually ask about the 'man from the *Telegraph*'. At that point you simply point vaguely towards the bar and say "He's the one at the bar with the beer stain on his tie." It always works.

The "Meet my third, fifth and sixth best friends in the world" Gambit

Always introduce every journalist to The Client as if you had known him for 30 years. Give the definite impression that the only reason a journalist would think of attending a press conference is out of a close personal affection for yourself.

Reporters will rarely go to the trouble of pointing out that they have never seen you in their lives. It is even possible to make up interesting stories about good times you have had in the past. "Remember the night you drank 15 bottles of champagne in the Hilton in Helsinki?" or "The last time I saw you was the time we went hang-gliding off that cliff in Tahiti." These total fabrications will be accepted without question and probably embellished.

Once The Client has met the correspondent of the *Daily Express* (your second cousin, twice removed) he will feel that you have done your bit, just by conjuring him up.

It is rash to make any forecast of the coverage of the press conference. The story may sink without trace. ("Can't understand why it wasn't in the *Express*. You met the correspondent, didn't you?") Or it might just capture someone's imagination and be on the front page.

Whatever the outcome, act as though it is just what you expected.

Press Releases

Producing press releases is the most conspicuous part of the PR person's job, probably the only part that both The Client and the outside world will recognise as work.

It is vital that you originate a steady flow of material and send it to as many journals and programmes as possible. This is not, as you might think at first, because it is the sort of effort that will help The Client get good publicity. This, if it happens, is a helpful side effect. The real reason is to prove that you are doing something.

To the company director, used to gauging the effectiveness of people's work by the number of flanged grommits they can produce in a day, the effectiveness of PR is judged by the number of press releases that are generated. Luckily press releases are considerably easier to fashion than flanged grommits.

The Golden Rules of Press Release Writing

1. The Client will never admit it, and you should never allude to it, but he is really only interested in seeing his name (and better still his photograph) in a paper that is read by his friends. There is no point in getting a full page in the *Financial Times* if everyone in The Client's local hostelry reads the *Uttoxeter Free Press*.

2. Include some deliberate mistake in any DRAFT that you submit for checking. A spelling mistake will do, though you could try a grammatical flaw, like a split infinitive, if The Client is that way inclined. Once he has corrected this, he will be convinced that he has written the entire press release himself.

3. Present your press release on one side of the paper, double-spaced and with huge margins. You patiently explain to The Client that this is to enable the subs on the newspaper to edit your copy. The real reason is that it makes it look as though you have done more work. As well as judging you by the number of press releases, The Client will also go by the length of each one, even though no more than the first two paragraphs are likely to be printed.

4. Use a word processor to write your press release. This makes it much easier to rehash old releases. Many old hands in agencies have got through life with only three or four. Use the find-and-replace facility on the word processor to pull out the old company name and put in the new one.

   Some brazen operators will submit the same press release to The Client over and over again without it ever being noticed (remember to change the date). The Client becomes convinced that you are becoming a better and better writer because each time he reads through a press release of yours there are fewer and fewer mistakes to correct.

5. Write your press releases in a style that appeals to The Client rather than to a newspaper or magazine sub-editor. Tell The Client that you are doing the exact opposite. Then if anyone objects to anything about your style you superciliously point out that "That's the way we write in newspapers."

   It is, of course, impossible to write in a newspaper or magazine style. For instance, a press release will read:

Acne Nails Ltd., Britain's leading carpentry accessory manufacturer, has revolutionised the 3½ inch nail market with a spectacular development in wood penetration technology – the product of 25 years of constant research and development.

The Acne 3½ inch Hold 'n' Hit SupaNail is generally accepted by every renowned nail expert in Western Europe as the greatest breakthrough in nail design since the launch of the Acne 3 inch SupaNail last month.

This will be changed by the sub-editor of the *Hammer User's Weekly* to:

'Acne Nails has launched a 3½ inch nail, which, they claim, has a new design.'

Everyone knows that this is the style used in newspapers but, frankly, you won't get away with a press release written like that.

6. Put in a quote from the person commissioning the press release. 'An authority on the nail market said today . . .' Give the impression that this is from a leading expert and that he actually knows what he is talking about. By definition this means making it up yourself.

7. Take a suitable length of time to produce a press release. The actual time taken to write the copy can vary from 90 seconds to anything up to four and a half minutes. This must be kept a deadly secret. Just as people place a value on possessions based on how much was paid for them, those who can't write will

value the time and effort far more than the quality. So never let anyone see any writing until it has matured on your desk for about three days – then don't forget to complain what a rush it was.

Who Wants to Know?

Press releases are becoming far too easy to send out, so that a whole host of non-bluffers are flooding the media with their pedestrian verbiage. The press distribution agency will supply a catalogue listing publications and broadcast programmes that you have never even thought of, so that, by filling in an extra code or two, you decide you might as well send to them.

Any journalist who has shown the slightest response to a previous release (such as informing you that you have got something wrong) will go on to your master press list and continue to receive even the most trivial announcements in perpetuity.

Ripeness is All

Clients love the embargo. ('For use on or after 00.01 hours, GMT, Friday 31 February.') It is as though you were dictating to the journalists just how and when they should handle the information that The Client has deigned to release.

The Client also loves the idea of an exclusive. A journalist will persuade him that she alone loves the company and truly understands. Don't bother about the others, she says. Just give the story to her and she will give it a big splash.

When the day comes, she will find a story she likes

better and, if yours is topical, you will have lost everything. Or The Client, who has insisted on the embargo in the first place, will allow her to break it. She runs the story first and nobody else will touch it.

The embargo should be for the convenience of the journalist not The Client, so that a 200-page report does not have to be summarised in the ten minutes before the copy deadline. Releasing the story simultaneously to a wide list enables you to hedge your bets, relying on the swings and roundabouts that are so important to the bluffer.

We do not advise telephoning correspondents to ask what they think of your press release. They might tell you. That is, if they think anything at all.

With all the bumf that they receive, they are most likely to have lost it. When you phone round for responses to your invitation to a press conference *all* journalists will swear they have never received it.

There will be agitation at the other end of the phone, a mounting panic which has nothing to do with the subject of your press conference. Every journalist is haunted by the thought of the one magic piece of paper, at last carrying a startling revelation, which everybody else has received and he has not.

"Describe it," he will often say. "Describe it!"

"Well," you say, "it has a red triangle in the top right-hand corner and a blue strip at the bottom . . ."

"Oh *that*," he says, losing interest immediately. "Yes, I have received *that*."

A journalist we know on the *Church Times* was telephoned by a well-spoken lady, acting as PR for a charity. It had to be confessed that their release had been mislaid.

"Let us all keep deadly calm," said the tight-lipped voice on the line.

Local Angle

There is seldom a story so banal that it does not fill a gap for somebody somewhere.

A host of radio stations around the country will welcome a high-quality tape of the person you are promoting as an 'authority', as long as it is free and does not mention the product. (The Client may be a bit awkward about this, since he has paid for the studio time, plus a percentage.) Remember that, in the continuous chatter of local radio, no supposedly serious subject lasts for more than two minutes. That is not counting the phone-ins, which last forever.

Everybody swears by one trade paper. If it's in there, it must be true. And the writer of its light-hearted gossip column is desperate for anything on the subject which has not been said before.

Media Events

Media events allow you to do lots of things that you want to do and use the press as an excuse for doing them. This might sound difficult but The Client will probably conspire to make it happen because he wants to do the same things too.

So when it is suggested that you launch the company's new five centimetre left handed screw, you suggest the best way to do this is to take a bunch of journalists on a five day all-expenses paid trip to Tahiti.

Now you know and he knows that there is no logical reason why you should launch the left handed screw in Tahiti. But its amazing how quickly you can create a case to persuade the board an expenditure like this is justified – especially if you make it plain that they will all have to attend too.

For a start you point out that you will be sure to get all the top editors and journalists to go. Don't mention that you could probably get the same people on the promise of a pie and a pint and a pen with the company logo on it. No-one wants to hear such nit-picking details.

You say that this will allow the company to have a full five days of these journalists' undivided attention; that the only slight distractions the press party might have are lounging on the beach, swimming, drinking, eating and going to night clubs.

Then you slip into the conversation that it will certainly outclass your main competitor who took the same people on a three day, all-expenses paid trip to Wolverhampton.

Factory Visits

Factory visits will often be suggested by The Client's accountant who will point out that the same results achieved by a five day spree to Tahiti could be obtained with a half-day visit to the company's Sunderland plant and a pie and pint in the pub round the corner.

He may produce his own reasons for this, such as:

a) it will allow the press to actually see the left-handed screws being made

b) it will not involve the entire board disappearing for a week

c) it will cost the company around £14.35 (excluding VAT).

This must be countered immediately. You do so by whole-heartedly agreeing with his suggestion and start making plans.

First you point out that the plant and its workforce will need a little tarting up. To give the right impression the company will have to issue the workforce with new overalls. Better still, this would be a good opportunity to initiate the changes recommended in your Corporate Image plan and decide on a new uniform for the workforce. Suggest the chairman's wife should come in every day for the next three months to look at colours and designs.

Then the entire factory will need redecoration, the equipment will have to be cleaned and the pin-ups will have to be removed (this alone could result in three days' lost production because of the strikes).

The bits of the factory that are actually falling down will have to be rebuilt at a cost of no more than £750,000. Three thousand trees and shrubs will have to be planted around the building to hide cracks in the walls and cover the output pipe where they pump the effluent into the river. Better still, they should really build the effluent treatment plant they were supposed to have built five years ago: "You don't want the journalists ignoring the left handed screws and writing their entire story about how environmentally unfriendly the company is, do you?"

And of course, they will need to dispose of the lathe operator who shouts abuse at any visitors. Point out that the only reason it hasn't been done before is that his brother is the shop steward.

Ask the accountant to cost this operation including lost production time. Then go home and pack your cases for Tahiti.

IN-HOUSE PR

Perhaps the happiest situation is that of the in-house PR person who has only one individual to confuse: his employer. Obviously you have to pick this employer carefully. Here are a few personality traits that are worth looking out for:

a) an overpowering belief that he has 'made it' if he sees his name in a newspaper

b) an almost paranoid fear of talking to reporters

c) dyslexia.

Once appointed, there are one or two basic rules of behaviour that you should follow. These can be applied to any office job but they are particularly useful in public relations.

1. A moving target is always hardest to hit. Never be at your desk. It is far better to sit through a matinée of old Hammer Horror movies than to be visible in your office all afternoon. If you are not there, colleagues will assume that you are out and about relating to the public in some way that they are not capable of imagining. By contrast, if people see you sitting at your desk day after day, they will quickly start wondering what you are doing. This could be fatal. It also means that you have to be pretending to work all day long which is very tiring.

2. Unless you have arranged a meeting, never speak to anyone in your company face to face. Always call on your car phone on the way to somewhere. This can mean popping down to the car park in order to speak to someone in the next office but you will quickly find that the effort is worth while.

Don't be tempted to make the calls from your office using a tape recording of traffic noise to give the impression of being on the move. Your car phone bill will not be as it should be. This is very dangerous, as it might mean they will think that you don't need a car phone and take it away.

3. Never be seen drinking alone. If you are observed in a bar all day continually buying drinks for a bunch of reprobates, everyone will presume that you are doing your duty. If anyone spots you in a pub at lunch time drinking a half pint of beer on your own, they will instantly assume you are an alcoholic. Drinking orange juice at a press conference will mark you out as an alcoholic also. Better to choose the sparkling tonic which might or might not contain a vodka.

4. Never stay in a company (or an agency) too long. It is important that you should change your job about every 18 months. It is possible to team up with three or four other PR people and work a rota system, so that you can come back to the same company every eight or nine years.

5. Never, ever be tempted to try to do the job without bluffing. The 'work' looks easy. But if you try to take it seriously it can be absolutely exhausting.

Paraphernalia

Your office should be smart and functional and packed with computers, laser printers, plotters, faxes, modems, intercoms, cellular phones and any other kind of expensive device you can think of. The only reason why the company has acquired a PR function in the first place is because there is an unspoken conviction that money spent on the means of communication will make up for the fact that there is nothing to communicate.

Top executives like to 'invest' in elaborate equipment, especially if they do not know precisely what it is for. 'Capital expenditure' is something they feel very comfortable with.

It is essential that you should switch on all this equipment every morning and that you should never be caught playing Space Invaders.

Meetings

A vital weapon in the in-house bluffer's armoury is the ability to call meetings. Arrange to have meetings on the flimsiest excuse and rope in as many people as possible. Have them over lunch (or better still breakfast) and get sandwiches brought in. This gives the impression that you are so busy that you could not contemplate not working through meal times.

If you hold meetings on a regular basis you can guarantee to put off 95 per cent of all decisions until the next one. This is nothing to do with bluffing, by the way. It is what happens in business meetings where people are not even trying to bluff. Remember that the modern company man lives for and through meetings. Conforming to this apparently aberrant behaviour will make you seem trustworthy.

Because public relations is much more exciting and romantic than production targets and profit margins and all the tedious things they usually talk about, a feeling of fun and eagerness pervades the public relations' meetings. Top executives have been known to smile anything up to three or four times within the space of two hours.

Don't be tempted to try to get anything resolved or decided at meetings. They are not really for that. They are more a sort of corporate encounter therapy. Some of the best meetings are the ones where you just work out an agenda for another meeting. Put some thought into creating good, regular meetings that can be held every week or fortnight; titles like 'Media Planning Meeting' or 'New Product Campaigns Think-Tank' look very good in your diary and don't usually produce much work for you to do.

Of course you have to explain that the reason for the meeting is to give everyone a chance to have 'an input to the creative process'. To do this you are best to embark upon some hopelessly futile venture – say preparing a **corporate brochure**. Rather than write the copy yourself (an exercise that would take about 35 minutes) you can stretch it out to two or three years by setting up a working party and 'taking on board' everyone's 'creative input'.

By the time this process is complete the copy for the brochure will be hopelessly out of date and you can quite justifiably start another series of meetings.

In-house Magazine or Newspaper

There are three kinds of story that are needed for this kind of publication:

1. The story that shows the Chairman/Managing Director is an all-round interesting individual. Its content is not too important, really. Not compared with the colour picture of the great man, and, if possible, his wife.

2. A story explaining how good the company is. This is usually a press release that you put out to the media last week.

3. A story demonstrating how the company looks after its employees. It is important that the ones chosen should look totally inept and unemployable.

There are also, of course, two further essential stories:

– A story explaining how well the company is doing in some exotic location – the Bahamas or Peru. Do not be concerned about the fact that your company doesn't do any business in the Bahamas or Peru. You will have to research and write this yourself, naturally.

– A story explaining how much publicity the public relations effort is getting the company.

Corporate Identity

Corporate identity is summed up in the philosophy 'If it doesn't move, stick a company logo on it; if it moves, get it to wear a company tie.' As a philosophy, this is pretty simple. It is up to the PR bluffer to make it sufficiently complicated.

Getting to this position does not happen by chance, however. It takes a great deal of planning. First you have to persuade the management that their company cannot survive without an identity.

This is, of course, patently absurd. Few companies have an identifiable identity, including a number that have spent several million pounds trying to acquire one. Yet strangely enough this never occurs to executives.

When initiating a new company logo point out that:

a) it creates an immediately recognisable image

b) it gives a business-like impression to company literature

c) it engenders group feeling amongst employees, giving them a symbol to embody all that they are striving for in terms of quality, commitment and service.

The real reason is slightly different. You commission a new company logo because it means that you have to revamp and reprint every tiny piece of company literature – work that will keep you and any number of others fully employed for years.

Don't be tempted to sketch out a company logo yourself when you have a free half hour on a Sunday afternoon. Go to a design consultancy and get them to charge three quarters of a million pounds to have their top creative man or woman think up a logo when they have a free half hour on a Sunday afternoon.

The board will never appreciate a logo unless they have paid an inordinate amount of money for it. They will only believe a design is worth while if it is presented to them by somebody who has already been paid half a million pounds to create one for another company.

Policing a company identity is the only chance that PR people get to bully others in the company. If anyone dares to try to do any sort of publicity on their own account, you can pin them to the wall because they did not use the right typeface or because they used the wrong shade of colour in the company logo. There is no breaking of the rules too minor to merit the full weight of the corporate identity rule book.

When you find the slightest misdemeanour, you should, at the very least, rush off a memo (with a copy to every member of the board) saying "Did head office spend half a million pounds on a corporate image plan just to have you ignore it?" There is, of course, no sensible answer to a question like that.

The idea of creating uniformity throughout their little empire holds an uncanny fascination for businessmen. If you get the job as head of the secret police, just think what fun you can have.

Sponsorship

As the person who handles PR you constantly get passed the letters that read 'We wondered if a big company like yours could see its way to sponsoring the Curry Rivel 23rd Girl Guides under twelves cricket team. For only £12.50 we would be happy to have your company name tattooed on the faces of the entire team.' A standard letter is necessary to deal with such situations, one which takes 35 words to say "Sod off."

You will want to get involved in sponsorship deals, but only in ones that mean The Client forking out several hundred thousand pounds at a time for maximum publicity. Try a highly successful rugby club (Union not League), a round-the-world racing yacht, a Grand Prix racing team, a snooker or a tennis tournament. Don't be tempted to back a struggling, up and coming team or event, even if cheap. In public relations saving money is a distinct disadvantage.

From a business point of view sponsorship deals are an expensive way of getting free tickets to top sporting events. You can then invite all your main customers and look smug when the winners talk to you after the game/race/event. It is therefore a good idea to pick a sport that you (and the company chairman) like watching.

Avoid real tennis, amateur wrestling, or skittles, and do not give money to charities, no matter how deserving. They can never get tickets to any sporting occasions worth watching.

Damage Limitation

A major reason for employing PR people is for the protection given in the process of damage limitation. However, the only real protection given by the damage limitation is the job security it can give a PR bluffer. This is because the very thought of damage limitation worries The Client no end and confirms them in the view that they cannot live without a good PRO.

You can help to fan the damage limitation paranoia by sending the occasional gruesome story about a competitor or related industry to the MD attaching a note saying "Lucky it's not us."

If the worst happens and you are required to fend off the media, here are a few replies that could be adapted to suit any contingency:

a. How would you like to meet for a drink?

b. Have you ever visited our plant in the Bahamas?

c. If you think that's bad, do you know what our main competitor is doing?

d. Having heard that, all I can say is I'm just glad I handed in my notice this morning.

e. You have the basic facts there, but how much would you be prepared to pay for the *real* inside story?

PR CONSULTANT

Whether operating as an independent consultant, or as a member of a big agency, you will spend the majority of your time trying to get New Business.

Presentations

Starting out on your own, you will need, for your Presentation to a prospective client, some out-of-work actors to play the Chairman and Managing Director of your 'consultancy' (though in fact you are still operating from your garage) and your specialist Iron Filings Advisor. They will be introduced as The Team which, operating as a Think Tank, has come up with some firm recommendations concerning the future of ball bearings and how they should be 'perceived' by the nation.

You need the actors because the big international consultancy against which you are pitching will produce all these characters. Whoever gets the account, neither in your case nor in theirs will The Client ever see any of these people again.

If the big consultancy gets it, The Client, telephoning after three months and transferred from one extension to another, will be lucky if he can trace anyone he has dealt with before, except the trainee who took notes at the Presentation and now claims to be the Account Director but does not seem quite sure which client he is talking to. The members of The Team are probably all out at another Presentation. (Their iron filings advisor is today being described as an ichthyologist.)

Your method of Presentation, like that of the big consultancy, will be to treat the prospective client as an imbecile, because that is what is expected of you. Act as though you were a primary school teacher, with a big box of tricks to show that learning can be *fun*.

There will be an overhead *and* a slide projector and a screen to go with them, a pad of flip charts and a big television-style apparatus which nobody knows how to work. The members of The Team will all be needed simply to carry the stuff in. They will each make suggestions as to what the others should have done with the television apparatus.

You put forward your ideas one sentence (sometimes one word) at a time, and each one has its own page on the flip chart or its own slide on the screen. The television apparatus will cause each picture or set of words to break up into stars or stripes, when you have done with it, or to disappear to the right or left at random until everyone becomes uneasy and does not know what is going to happen next.

All these special effects are aids to the bluffer. They create an environment of doubt and confusion, so that you have room to manoeuvre and, using full opportunism, can move in any direction that seems likely to lead to success. When you know what the prospective client wants, you can scrap all the ideas in the Presentation.

Proposals

You will require just one master set of proposals, adapted for each occasion and produced late at night in frantic photocopying to be left behind after the Presentation or not, according to how well your ideas have been received.

Whether the prospective client is Tristan da Cunha Airlines or the Bank of the Isle of Wight, what you propose will be more or less the same. You will demonstrate:

- What is to be said
- Who it is said to
- How it is said.

The activities you try to sell will also be similar. They will include **seminars** (a few people talking around a table) and one-to-one meetings (i.e. **lunches**) between The Client and a Key Figure. There will be a **brochure** to Tell The Client's Story and **media events** to gain the company *the recognition that it deserves*.

Costs

A breakdown of what it will all cost generally comes right at the end of the proposals. Sophisticated potential clients are getting to know this and sometimes jokily open them at the back. It is worth fooling them by making the very last section a Pollyanna vista of the far-off future in which consultancy and client alike emerge into the sunlight.

Since you do not know how much The Client is prepared to spend, or what your competitors are charging (though you may be sure the proposals of your competitors will all be the same as yours), what you do is fog the issue. Set out a series of sums which add up to a total that frightens The Client out of his wits. You know you are not going to get that. You yourself will laugh at it at the Presentation. But you aim to get The Client to buy as many as possible of the separate components and at least to put off considering the rest. You have in mind, because it is your own bread and butter, a minimum figure below which you cannot subsist.

Especially if you are a starter bluffer, do not always go for the mammoth fees. You would have to hire all those out-of-work actors to service the account. A big fee could just be the opportunity to lose money on a larger scale.

Percentages

Forget about ten and twenty per cent: have some really convincing figures, like 5.85 per cent and 17.65 per cent. Nobody would make these up.

Advertising agencies receive (or did receive) a discount of 15 per cent on the rates for newspaper space or air time. You, as a PR consultant, have paid out the full amount of £100 for, let us say, photographic prints.

The percentage of 17.65 is more or less what you have to add so that, when 15 per cent of the new total is deducted, it comes back to the amount you paid in the first place. (There is a blank page at the end of the Guide for you to work this out.)

The figure of 5.85 per cent of the fee is what one agency found it was spending on stationery, photocopying, telephoning and postage, all routine expenses related to the amount of work that was done. Adding 5.85 per cent is certainly cheaper than the time needed to count every piece of paper. Most clients surrender.

It is hard for a bluffer to admit, but there is sense in all this. If you do not reclaim your out-of-pocket expenses, it means that, the more active you are, the less you will earn.

Clear Head for Figures

If you are going to make a living out of bluffing, money is the one area in which you will need to keep a clear head. Muzziness in all other aspects of public relations is regarded as the normal atmosphere in which to conduct yourself.

We can save you from one or two pitfalls into which novice bluffers, devil-may-care by nature, have tumbled in the past.

1. The first delusion is to quote a 'global' sum to cover both your fees and the money that you will pay out. You draw a figure out of the air which seems enormous at the time but you will live to regret it.

   Bluffing eats money. The more tendentious and tedious the story, the more elaborately The Client will want it gift-wrapped into glossy brochures and videos with a cast of thousands. All of these will cost.

2. The second snare is to quote an all-round fee to cover all your time in the year ahead, allowing The Client as much as he can eat for, say, £99,743.

It is amazing how long each project will take to complete when it comes to the point, especially if you are learning how to do it as you go along.

As you develop that hearty relationship with The Client, he will call on you for all sorts of chores that you had not even dreamed of. When you suggest an extra fee for all this additional 'work', he will remind you that you promised the earth in your proposals.

And indeed you did. You gave him the impression that you would take him totally into your care, obeying his slightest whim and solving all his fancied 'problems', some of which you had helped him to fancy.

That old bluff, the Retainer, appears to be a thing of the past. It was money for old rope, a sum you charged simply for breathing or for 'being at the end of a

43

telephone', as old-style PR consultants used to put it, meaning the call box at the Wig and Pen Club.

You now make a virtue of not quoting an initial Retainer, to be billed in advance before the meter even starts ticking. Regrettably, you can no longer charge The Client just for loving him.

Time, Please

What you have to be paid for is the time that you have put in. If you are a freelance, it will take you as long to get the work as to do it. So your fee must support you for twice the time that each project occupies.

We naturally expect you to expand so that you are soon transformed into A. Bluffer *and Associates* with your wife and great-uncle (a retired accountant) on the board. (A. Bluffer *and Partners* means that you are living irregularly with goodness knows how many people.)

Once you are working with other bluffers and for more than one Client, you will need to keep rigid time sheets. That hour and a half this morning that you spent looking for a lost document: which client's document was it, whether you found it or not? He will have the time clocked up against him.

Time spent in general muddle, or in organising this Friday's farewell party, goes down as Administration, which means it comes out of your own pocket. This is bad. But, in a big consultancy, whenever you cannot remember what you did, the time goes down as New Business. This is held to be good.

Because of Overheads, Administration and New Business, if your consultancy is going to make even a modest profit, you will have to charge everyone's hours at three times their salary rate.

When charging the hours to The Client, you will have one rate for yourself as an 'experienced' consultant, another for the lady who is word-processing (and is in fact running the place) and a smaller one for the young man with a First in Theology from Oxford who is doing the photocopying.

If words get processed, that is nothing to what happens to figures as you contemplate further break-downs and groupings. We do not mean that you will cook the books. The amounts will be as they should. They will add up to what they must. As you bluff along your way, it is all a matter of what you call things.

Tomorrow the World

No consultant can stay in business these days without claiming to advise internationally. This presents challenges.

On the Continent of Europe, the trouble is the languages. In New Zealand and Australia, they use the English language but with such directness that it is difficult to find room for the nuances of bluffing. In the United States, they use it so carelessly that it is a shame to take the money. In Canada, you are required to bluff simultaneously in two languages, a skill akin to juggling. Bluffing, by its very nature, loses a lot in translation.

Your best stratagem is to keep constantly on the move and not remain in any country for more than two days. You then become an expert on that country, with 'first-hand' experience, though its Holiday Inn does seem eerily similar to all the others you have stayed in.

And be sure to tell everybody, as you set off with your Club Class ticket, that you really detest travelling.

Anybody else would be welcome to go in your place, you declare as you slam the taxi door and set off for the airport.

For the benefit of your consultancy, you will want to establish mutual back-scratching agreements with agencies in various countries who are as hungry for business as you are so that you will be able to list the capitals of these countries on your letterhead.

In some Latin countries, your associate consultant will assure you that you have to bribe journalists. You will simply refuse. Bluffing is one thing; corruption is another.

From those who have tried bribery, the sequence, not to anyone's surprise, goes like this. If you are holding a press conference, your associate consultant tells you to allocate a sum of money which he will hand to the President of, let us say, the Association of Motoring Correspondents. Before you have even decided to do so, the President himself arrives at your hotel.

"Don't give the money to that old rogue," he says. "He keeps half of it. Give it all to me."

He has no sooner departed than individual motoring correspondents start telephoning. "Don't give it to the President" is their theme. "He keeps two-thirds of it. Give it all to us."

All the correspondents come along to the press conference, mainly to haggle with each other and with you. They go away bearing rich gifts. The next day there is not a line in the papers.

"It is simple," one of the correspondents will explain to you charmingly afterwards. "There was no story. If there had been a story, you could have faxed it to the wire service and everybody would have printed it."

FINANCIAL RELATIONS

It is strange that many a bluffer, confident of mastering abstruse subjects such as electronic engineering or molecular biology after a few quick dives into the encyclopaedia, will draw back from Finance out of a misplaced sense of awe.

But this applies in any specialised field and, if you are the keen bluffer we think you are, you should have learned to keep matters vague enough to avoid exposure. Remember that if you are bluffing, the fund managers and investment analysts are bluffing too, not to mention the finance directors of quoted companies and the Chairman. They have simply been at it longer and know how to produce a better smokescreen and to hedge their forecasts more skilfully. Such people are worth studying.

Annual Report

A good place to start is the **Annual Report**. Steer clear of all those figures in the Balance Sheet and the Source and Application of Funds. These must be left to the accountants who will employ a style of bluffing which frankly is not for the beginner. It takes years to train such people. They even have to sit exams.

You could start by calling up a few bar charts illustrating results over the past ten years. Because of accumulating inflation, these will show an upward trend, certainly in research expenditure, probably in sales and possibly in profits. You can also commission some colour photographs. Remember that even ball bearings and iron filings can be made to look glamorous as long as they are artistically lighted.

Never mind the Profit and Loss and all those Notes to

the Accounts, though the small print of these, showing how the figures have been cooked and the funds laundered, constitute the only informative part of the whole glossy production. Your true province is the Chairman's **Annual Review** which, of course, the Chairman is too busy to write. If he is a Non-Executive Chairman, he may in fact be forbidden to write it. This is where you step in.

All you need to know is whether it has been a Good Year or a Bad Year. If it has been a Good Year (e.g. if profits have risen more or less in line with the industry average) this is due to the enterprise and acumen of the Chairman, the tireless efforts of the Board (who would like to thank all members of staff) and to far-sighted, long-term planning. If it has been a Bad Year, this is due to government intervention, unrealistic wage claims, unfair foreign competition and the world economic climate.

The only section of the Annual Report that most people will read is the section containing the Chairman's salary or, better still, his 'remuneration' which is three times as much.

Inside Information

Maynard Keynes, who made a pile on the stock market, said that you have to buy or sell not on what you think but on what you think people will think. Helping people to think the unthinkable is what you are there for.

Fundamentally there is only one source for any real clue as to how a company is doing and that is the company itself. Once upon a time, a company would only release its results annually and not always then if it could help it. Now a **half-year report** is obligatory and **quarterly reports** are favoured by some. It all means 'work' for you.

You will have to be careful not to appear to be cashing in on 'inside information' yourself. Knowing the company as you do, you can see that it is virtually impossible, even for insiders, to get hold of any information at all. Usually it is as much as you can do to get anyone to tell you the time.

You have to be sure that all 'price-sensitive' information is made available equally to everybody at the same moment. See that the quarter's figures go first to the Stock Exchange. After that, you can do what you like, except change the inexorable figures. Well, more or less what you like. It would not be a bad idea to study the regulations. The Client might go to prison if you do the wrong thing and so might you, though you have to keep explaining to people that this would be outside your 'terms of reference.'

Nobody wants to know about the ball bearings and iron filings themselves, but, if it is about the company's financial prospects (what people are going to think), every small announcement, such as the final retirement of the President Emeritus, will be pounced upon and all sorts of trends read into it.

The investment analysts will write a Letter to the clients of the stockbroker for whom they work, advising them to buy or sell shares in The Client's company (whichever it is the stockbroker does not care). Then the financial columns will quote what the analyst says and other analysts will take note of what the financial columns say and the whole game will be kept going a treat.

Just to show some action to The Client, you could organise, at the time that suits you best, an **open day** for financial journalists in the research laboratories.

They will not learn anything that they did not know before (they may tell the Research Director a few things about the international scene) but they are sure to come to a conclusion (Buy, Sell or Hold in almost equal proportions.) And they will study every augury, including the weather.

Keeping in Funds

The people you need to confuse the most will be the Fund Managers of the insurance companies, the pension schemes and the unit trusts which own the greater part of The Client's company and which are in a much stronger position to put pressure on it than the little old ladies who were the shareholders of yesterday.

The managers of the funds, staking tens of millions of pounds, do not themselves own a piece of the action. They get their reward in the form of lush lunches at the daily **Road Shows** of the type which you yourself can stage manage. At the Road Show, the Chief Executive Officer and the Chief Financial Officer of your client's company will use a plethora of graphs and charts, videos and multi-screen presentations to demonstrate that the company's present indifferent performance is no real indication of its glorious future.

You will want to take the Road Show out of London to Edinburgh or to the other outlying financial centres of the country in which you are operating. There are not many investment analysts, fund managers and financial journalists in these places but it doubles and trebles the 'work'.

GOVERNMENT RELATIONS

For a few pounds you can acquire Roth's *Parliamentary Profiles* which contains full details of every MP ('fat, bald-headed old beezer'), and all the Issues with which he has been identified. As long as The Client does not get hold of this volume, you will be able to bring the name of any MP into the conversation as if he was known to you.

Like the world of finance, the arena of politics contains many apparent mysteries which evaporate as soon as you move into it yourself. You trust The Client will not have the time to do so, and that his illusions will consequently remain intact. He will be eager to flood MPs with information to show how oppressed his company is and will believe that iron filings are the only subject that ought to be on their minds.

The trick is to approach the MPs one by one, looking for a constituency or a subject interest, maybe an aunt who is a ball-bearing roller. The advantage to the bluffer is that this takes up more time. MPs are happy to be contacted if they think there is a vote in it somewhere. The opportunity to get to know them arises when their party is in opposition. They are then sorely missing the official cars, the staff to brief them, and all the attention that they receive when in government.

It is possible to obtain the printed House of Commons telephone directory which contains the direct-line numbers of all MPs and their secretaries. We recommend you to try the secretaries first. The MPs themselves sometimes get a bit shirty.

Parliament itself is old hat. Anybody can see it on television. There are from time to time several Select Committees sitting which are open to the public. Just tell the policeman at the public entrance which one you are going to and walk in. (Watch for opportunities as you pass through the Central Lobby.)

These committee sessions are often small affairs. You may find you are the only person in the chairs for the public. When the session is over, the MPs tend to stand around and chat for a bit. It is comparatively easy to go up to one of them and invite him or her to meet The Client. You can write to the Clerk of the Committee and they just might invite The Client to give evidence at a future session. In which case you will have a field day. As always, it is worth a try.

PQs

You can arrange to receive the formidable wad of papers that MPs thumb through every morning. These contain the Parliamentary Questions (you must call them PQs) put down for the days to come. The Client may well know the answer to one of them ("To ask the Secretary of State how many left-handed iron filers are employed in Rutland and if he will make a statement"). If so, he may or may not wish to help out the Secretary of State by telling him.

For your part, you or The Client can get in touch with the MP who put down the question and can gratify any interest that he or she has in the industry. (Don't assume that the putting down of the question implies that the MP has any.) More to the point, you can find out who is prompting him or her to ask it. You can prompt an MP yourself by suggesting further questions to be put down, preferably those that will put The Client's competitor in a bad light.

MPs suffer the embarrassment of having all their improvised bluffing recorded in Hansard. They are

expected suddenly to become indignant about whichever topic comes into prominence from day to day. Out
of their depth, as you are, they are often desperate
for facts. Churchill's 'one side of one sheet of paper' is
what they will be looking for and this is what will earn
their regard.

Obedient Servants

It is not long before you learn that what takes place in
parliament does not really alter anything. A lot of what
is said is simply for show. Meanwhile the mechanism of
government has got to grind on. Such action as there is
will come from civil servants.

It is a civil servant, racing around the corridors of the
Department, who drafts the answer to the PQ for the
Secretary of State to deliver. A little jury box of civil
servants sits in the debating chamber, ready at any
time to straighten Ministers out.

You can buy from Her Majesty's Stationery Office the
Civil Service Year Book which lists the name, the
function and the direct line telephone number of every
official of any note in each Department of State (and
many other governmental bodies). When you have
tracked down the iron filings 'desk' in the Department
of Trade and Industry, the person answering the phone,
who lives and breathes iron filings like The Client, will
be much more ready to tell you what is happening than
would the Department's information officers.

And the specialist civil servant will be as ready to
absorb factual information as to give it. It all provides
'input' for their quota of documentation, those multitu-
dinous 'papers' for Permanent Secretaries and Ministers to shelve.

Issues

Much of your government relations work will consist of
providing The Client with 'parliamentary intelligence',
identifying the **issues** which otherwise he will not
recognise until they hit him. Broadly speaking, an
'issue' is any movement or measure that will stop his
company doing whatever it pleases.

When legislation is mooted that would make life
difficult for The Client, your technique will be to
demonstrate that it cannot be enforced. The people to
tell are the civil servants, for they are the ones who will
have to operate it and it may make life even more
difficult for them. If there is one thing a civil servant
enjoys it is a quiet life.

European Dimension

Once you have attained the pinacle of in-house Director
of Public Affairs, you will want to establish a tiny office
in Brussels to which you can fly when the heat becomes
too intense at headquarters. Apart from the good food,
the attraction of European Relations is that the
Commission positively welcomes lobbying. It wants to
hear from everybody and aims to complicate matters
much as you do yourself but on a scale you have never
dreamed of. It blends irreconcilable points of view into
documents with the texture of sliced bread.

Get to Europe early, for the Directives of the next
decade are already in the pipeline. Green papers and
consultative documents will be discussed and amended
and referred back and discussed again. Everyone else
making an 'input' will be bluffing, so you might as well
make one too.

WILDER SHORES OF BLUFF

Medical Public Relations

Medical public relations requires qualities of anti-bluff or, let us say, defensive play. With ball bearings or iron filings, you are building up each story for all that it is worth. By contrast, you have to devote all your efforts to stop a medical story from getting out of hand. It is not funny to see a minor technological advance labelled New Cure for The Common Cold.

Information, Please

In medical public relations, you can always initiate, for example, the In-Growing Toe Nails Information Bureau. A leaflet, written by a nurse, will show how as little as an hour a day of attention to the toe nails will keep them in good shape and prevent in-growing.

It will command enquirers to give up smoking because of the high correlation, postulated but not established, between even passive smoking and in-growing toe nails. It will enjoin them to drink nothing but milk. (A Healthy Diet Means A Healthy Nail.) The leaflet will carry a tiny line saying that it is published by The Client 'in the interests of sturdier toes'.

You send this leaflet to the writers of the medical advice columns of the women's magazines. They will invite readers to apply for it, free, at the address of your consultancy which happens to be the headquarters of twelve other information bureaux. You will send out the leaflet as promised but can also slip in to the envelope sales literature about those special scissors manufactured by The Client.

As in any other field, you will need some authoritative quotes. In the realm of medicine, these will come from our old friend 'a doctor'.

Two maxims are worth bearing in mind. One is that the most commonplace remark (Too Much Sun Burns The Skin) becomes news every time a doctor utters it. The other is that there is no statement so silly that you cannot find a doctor somewhere to say it.

Desk Research

As with so many words, when used in public relations, research does not mean whatever it says in the dictionary. It means simply ringing a few people up to ask what they think. You will learn to refer to this as **Desk Research**. Armchair Research would be more like it.

This is qualitative rather than quantitative research. You earnestly warn The Client that it is not 'statistically significant', trying to shield him from the realisation that it is not significant at all.

When you do ring round, it is amazing how soon the comments start to form into a pattern. Everybody knows what is wrong with the company, except, of course, the company itself.

These quotes, when lifted from the back of the envelope on which you have scribbled them, will not be attributed to any named individual but simply to 'an MP', 'a Senior Civil Servant' or 'a Middle-East Ambassador'. No need to point out the opportunities for bluffing there.

You copy out the quotes, 'analyse' them and tell The Client they point to the inescapable conclusion that he should do what you have been telling him to do all along.

Apart from this, The Client will often ask you to find out things. "You, with all your contacts, should be able to discover . . ." The golden rule is always to look first in the telephone directory. Does The Client want to know about the activities of a Pressure Group? They are probably listed. Ring them up and ask them. They will be pleased to tell you at great length all that they are up to.

We were once handling the official opening of a factory that made animal feed supplements. One of the products was a fish food. (Another was a pill that made flamingos pinker.)

The idea was to have a tank of large fish in Reception. They would be kept a little hungry for the occasion. The Chairman, instead of cutting a tape or unveiling a plaque, would sprinkle some granules on the surface. The fish would all rise, making a good picture.

We spent a whole afternoon on the telephone, seeking a firm that would hire us a large fish tank. (It is better than working for a living.) We tried Harrods. We tried Woolworths. We tried the local pet store. We tried the trade paper. The answer, when found, turned out to be a firm named Fish Tanks Limited. They were in the London phone book.

If you are looking for some precise information, try your local Reference Library. Librarians are miraculous at tracking down the answers as long as you know the questions to put to them. But don't expect them to do your bluffing for you; they are not trained for it. And they have this regrettable reverence for facts.

You will need to employ desk research on your own account when you are becoming an instant expert on a certain subject. A good source will be the professional body or trade association of whatever industry is involved.

It is staggering that people, when approached by a complete stranger, and an ignorant one at that, do not simply tell you to get lost. But everybody likes to talk about their work. Especially if you sound interested. In public relations it is necessary to accentuate the positive as never before. It becomes a bit wearisome at times.

Safety in Numbers

Of course there is still room for 'statistically significant' research on the lines of the opinion polls which seem now to have taken the place of elections. You can, for example, 'buy in' a couple of questions on **attitudes** to iron filings to be added to the regular opinion survey ("What do you think of the Prime Minister?") put to a cross-section of the populace every week.

Bluffing in **statistics** is a special skill but the intermediate bluffer can learn to sit in on a meeting and, while other people are talking, prove with a pocket calculator that the breakdowns of the breakdowns of the figures of someone else's research are 'within standard error', i.e. the answer is just as likely to be No as Yes.

Full-scale **opinion research**, paid for by The Client, can be the means of measuring what people think of the company and, after an interval of time, how your work has altered what they think.

It will be a brave bluffer who will take the survey to the second stage. Half a century ago, a bank in the United States discovered by research that customers were afraid of their bank manager.

So they took out the iron grilles, put in soft lighting and installed low, cosy counters with pretty girls sitting behind them who said "Hi!" A few years later, they repeated the research, scrupulously matched to be strictly comparable, and found that customers were *still* afraid of their bank manager.

Opinion Formers

It seems to have been some time in mid-century that the Americans invented the concept of Opinion Formers. They would send a glossy brochure on iron filings to every doctor and minister of religion throughout the land. Before that, they had been casting their message to the winds, trusting it would find a home somewhere.

The idea was that, if these pillars of society were satisfied with the motives of the company, their attitudes would affect those of the rest of the community. If the 'Thought Leaders' thought ball bearings were wonderful their patients and parishioners would think the same.

These days, the talk is of **Target Listing**. An army of drudges can, at The Client's expense, compile a list of all the individuals in the Target Audience in every country of the world. You start by thinking of all the cabinet ministers, junior ministers and senior civil servants who might at some time be touched by an iron filing.

In Britain, these might be in the Home Office, the Department of Trade and Industry, the Departments of Health and Social Security, the Department of Education and Science, the Overseas Development Administration and the Defence Ministry. This is before you have got on to the 'shadow' ministers, who cover the same areas for the Opposition.

Then there are constituency MPs and councillors of all local authorities in which a ball bearing is made; activists in consumer and single-interest groups; trade union officials; members of council of the Guild of Magnet Makers; presidents of Rotary; officers of flag rank in the Salvation Army . . . Pretty soon, you might as well be mailing the electoral rolls of the entire nation.

The names and addresses are all entered on a computer. The members of council, of course, will change every year. The junior ministers will change every week. Further vast expense can keep the list updated.

For ever afterwards, innocent people, scattered all over, will wonder why they keep hearing about iron filings and ball bearings. They had hitherto taken for granted that there was nothing at all wrong with these worthy products. Now that there is so much special pleading, it makes them wonder if that can be the case.

Opinion Formers may be going out of fashion, as the Thought Leaders did before them. Nowadays the talk is of Decision-Takers and Decision-Influencers. Decision-Takers are Prime Ministers, judges, generals, chiefs of police, dentists and all the individuals who influence our lives. In a democracy, Decision-Influencers are presumably all the rest of us.

Speech-Writing

The 'writing' part makes this sound like work. It isn't. It is simply thinking aloud; your own normal bluffing conversation put into someone else's mouth. It just sweats out of you. Take a few platitudes, a couple of vague notions and just add water.

We know of one American speech writer who confessed that, newly married, he had absent-mindedly got into bed and turned to his wife with "I would like to begin by saying how very happy I am to be with you tonight."

A trip to the library will reveal that Bartlett's *Familiar Quotations* has a highly useful subject index. This will make The Client appear extremely learned. ("Was it not Aristotle who said . . . ?") We don't know about the filings but there are sure to be some references to iron. You might need a Concordance to the Bible or to Shakespeare, but don't let's overdo it.

When first asked to give a talk, The Client will not have the vaguest concept of what he wants to say. Fear not. Just set down the first thoughts that come into your head, thump the draft stamp on them and send them off. He will react to these with such horror that he will at last produce his own ideas. Take notes of what he says on the phone, transcribe them and send it all back to him, confident that his wrath will have made up his mind.

When the speech you have written is being delivered, you can go and sit at the back to hear how it sounds. Then at the end you can clap and shout "Author!"

As a speech writer, you will have opportunties for quoting yourself and quoting yourself quoting yourself which should be a source of job satisfaction. One week you write a speech for the Chairman, the next you write one for the Director of Research. "Last week, in Northampton, our Chairman said . . . I think these are very telling words and most appropriate for our time."

The week after you write a speech for the Director of Personnel. "Last week, in Plymouth, our Director of Research quoted our Chairman as saying . . . Not only are these very telling words and most appropriate for our time, but it was particularly perspicacious of the Director of Research to quote them on this occasion."

There is no reason why this process should ever stop.

THE AUTHORS

Basil Saunders is a Fellow of the Institute of Public Relations. He served one stint as a Member of Council, and two more stints on the Professional Practices Committee. He believes that taking oneself over-seriously is the occupational hazard of public relations.

He was trained in bluffing by the (American) General Electric Company in New York and Schenectady where public relations was regarded with solemnity, even forty years ago.

Returning to the UK, he became Chief Bluffer to the British Institute of Management. He then ventured into consultancy to be initiated into the wielding of the DRAFT stamp by Tim Traverse-Healy (doyen of public relations in the UK if only on the strength of his invention of this technique); and was subsequently Head of Bluffing, Worldwide, for the Wellcome Foundation.

His standard lecture "Public relations: newest profession or oldest?", intended to take the myth out of the subject, seems to have cheered a few people.

Alexander Rae is a tired-looking Glaswegian freelance writer with a moustache. If he had a pound for every book he has written he would now have £3.50.

He was once the press officer for a multi-national industrial conglomerate but gave it all up so as to offer his services to more than one client. He lives in Somerset (when available) with a wife, two sons and a charismatic computer.

His ambition is to find time to write for a living.

THE BLUFFER'S GUIDES

Available at £1.99 and (new titles* £2.50) each:

Accountancy	Modern Art
Advertising	Motoring
Antiques	Music
Archaeology	The Occult
Astrology & Fortune Telling	Opera
Ballet	Paris
Bird Watching	Philosophy
Bluffing	Photography
British Class	Poetry
Champagne*	P.R.
The Classics	Public Speaking
Computers	Publishing
Consultancy	Racing
Cricket	Rugby
The European Community	Secretaries
Finance	Seduction
The Flight Deck	Sex
Golf	Skiing*
The Green Bluffer's Guide	Small Business*
Japan	Teaching
Jazz	Theatre
Journalism	University
Literature	Weather Forecasting
Management	Whisky
Marketing	Wine
Maths	World Affairs

These books are available at your local bookshop or newsagent, or can be ordered direct from the publisher. Prices and availability are subject to change without notice. Just tick the titles you require and send a cheque or postal order (allowing in the UK for postage and packing 28p for one book and 12p for each additional book ordered) to:

Ravette Books Limited, 3 Glenside Estate, Star Road, Partridge Green, Horsham, West Sussex RH13 8RA.